Time and Motion

Time and Motion:
New & Selected Poems

Julian Croft

PUNCHER & WATTMANN

First published in 2025
Published by Puncher & Wattmann
PO Box 279
Waratah NSW 2298

info@puncherandwattmann.com

**NATIONAL
LIBRARY**
OF AUSTRALIA

A catologue record for this book is available from The National Library of Australia.

ISBN   9781923099692

Cover image: Adrian Feint, *Afternoon Collaroy*, 1940, New England Regional Art Museum
Cover design by David Musgrave
Printed by Lightning Source International

Contents

from *Ocean Island*

from *After a War (any war)*

Time and Motion

Family Photos

1980 — Post-War Retrospective

The Art of War

from *Breakfasts in Shanghai*

Breakfast in Shanghai

In between the omelette and toast
I have this idea of the Locomotive Hotel in Currabubula,
not that I've ever been there,
I've seen it from the train between Tamworth and Werris Creek
in between the waiting room and the wooden loo
where a man died and his body wasn't found for six weeks:
things happen in between – between women, children,
between growing up and growing old, between one fuck and another
there's always this idea of the Locomotive Hotel its door open
the sun fixed like a deadly lemon at midday
and the train standing stock still.
Is it time, is there time to get out,
to have a quick drink,
a quick flirt with the publican's wife,
and that final quick piss in the wooden loo
before the train leaves?

In between the omelette and the toast I've paused.

Timetable

I caught the train each afternoon from Waratah to Civic,
each morning from Civic to Waratah;
twenty-five years later standing here at the end/beginning?
of a palindrome of years waiting for an engine
wide-eyed and smokestack high, or getting off
from one bluff-bummed, third-eyed, and dripping coal
you wonder where all those things were put in motion—
circles and ellipses, points of departure, trailing and facing
along the years, and you ask yourself if all leaving
is really a coming, and departures arrivals, whether
getting off at Civic was better than going right in,
or, letting the overbridge at Waratah flash past
and sitting tight, hanging on like grim death until
the train grinds slowly into that ultimate terminus
high in the northern tablelands, was what you really wanted?

The Junction, 1946

Behind the school a train line ran
which brought from possum pits a rake
of splintered wagons and a van,
on every hopper's side a sign:
mysterious letters sliding past to make
the first sentences we learnt to read:
John Darling, Jubilee, Pacific, Glebe.

And as I read I feel the train grind past,
taste in these letters smoke and steam,
and hear the wheel beat coldly on the line;
though for this alphabet of smoky dreams
a newer line is laid to guide them past,
those poems differently made up still read
John Darling, Jubilee, Pacific, Glebe.

Myself, 1959

Out on the lake fishing, early morning
perhaps a Sunday for the water's smooth
and sounds carry across ten parishes:

your line trails over sand
you smell your skin: salt and steel sun,
over the gunwale green nylon dips

into another world, and without warning
you see yourself wondering who fishes
in your world, Julian, what moves

beyond, below, what hand
is poised in shadows years on
to pluck this memory from your lips

to take from Sunday surfaces of glass
your image on the lake's design
where flesh and sounds once floated,

but my hand, ours, which jerked this line
brought you gasping into my boat, dead
in this air which floats upon the past.

The Cerf-Volant

Somewhere in the last fifteen years
there is a kite flying over a beach
and there at the end of the string
having followed the kite from miles away
are the two of you. Just as the two of you
somewhere at this moment miles away,
if you looked up to see this string
of words would see above the beach
my thoughts, riding the tugs and buffets of the years.

At the End of Memorial Drive

Brown's cottage is a parking lot now.
Bitumen, concrete curbing, and white lines
seal off the skillion workshop, the anyhow
growth of creepers and tea-trees making mines
and caves of plants where old Brown
had built his boards as snug as pitprops
in the wind-beaten bush, all grown
together in galvanised and vegetable knots.

Sand blows from Bar Beach burying everything.
I fight the wind to bring blunt scissors
and the saw to be set. There's a bell to ring,
you use an iron stave to stir him out, a bent figure
in black waistcoat, long weathered face and oil-stained hat.
He never wastes a word but takes the work in hand
and disappears into a forge of darkness that I felt
was wet as salt and smothering as sand.

But reset saws catch nails and scissors pins.
He died and dozers came. The tall fronds,
the trees, the bush, the red-breasted swifts, even
the galvo and the spiky grasses, all gone.
The coal face sheers where the asphalt's waters run
and shows its fossils there, and shards
of broken glass, and the memory of a scythe
he sharpened that I tried for size and cut my thumb.

D-Zug

Right from the ambiguous start
when in the wrench and snatch of coupling
the child called out
"the station's moving and we are standing still",

I'd never known which track my heart was on,
the up express, all stations down,
or where to get out
if the station's moving and we are standing still;

I wasn't sure if the crumpled face floating
backward, mirror or window, was my own
or yours, or to shout
it's the next train moving, I'm standing still,

but tonight, expressed down rival tracks
through air-conditioned night, I saw an orange globe
of warmth burn past, then out,
and I was moving, you were standing still.

a walk to the bogey hole

high tide and a big swell from far away
salt blows like a curtain in a southerly
the waves bang shut on the beach
the boy and I decide to be mug lairs
and make the break round the rocks to the point

rock shelf barebacked to the sea swept
by the surf fetching smack into the small of a cliff
scratching stones out of sandstone ribs
you run like hell here to dodge the greenwhite lash
over susan gilmour's naked sand to the gulf

dungeoned above us the two ends and bight of a cliff
horseshoe, biscuit bitten, a black stripe of coal,
noose tight the track winds round: spray, mud
slips under our feet, the wave gate slams at the end
where the ladder rises to the upper circle of cliff

pressed against white railings above morisset's bath
with wind and swell straining through the chains
the boy asked: why bogey hole? bogey to bathe and hole
because the convicts dug it. how? with picks in between waves
your great grandfather was the commandant's man

felon, constable, senior constable, overseer,
morning sun under the lip of a collapsing wave
then the surge through the still water of the basin
the two of us muddy at walk's end on a narrow ledge:
limpets growing on those streaming chains.

Fathers and Sons

Not of your body but your mind.

No nine months carried in your blood hutched
by the deep forces which walked laughed
ate made love then birth:
mark of the muscle still upon my hip.
No, none of those...
you cut and chipped away at the completed work
some image there you saw beyond the one
a mother's tongue could make-
father's would lick it into shape, irony, sarcasm,
the rendering of flesh into tallow
to drip into another candle mould;
thin tapers which light the dark hallway
since that time James staggered in the back door drunk
transported for a crime no one knows,
and here I am, feeling my way along,
the nine-year candle guttering in my hand
knowing I'll not find out, nor he as well
who'll grow to make his own wick dip and burn.
Those whom you love but cannot bear
as when a finger held out to test if it's still there
burns, long after skin and nose tell you the quickness of both,
you keep it there...then pick the scab,
repeat the words which echo through five childhoods
make the flame jump to show
white shock, burning tide of shame flood in a face.
Made of my mind, as I was made
the long maze of this corridor winds on.
We learn it each, one generation,
but neither God nor others' genes
has helped us find the door.

Letter to His Son for His Eleventh Birthday During an Absence in China

In farmers' land, damp with Summer
Reading, of course, Li Bai, I think of you.
Here the mulberry is green and the girls work
steaming cocoons in the silk factory,
the rain softens the earth and the three sleeps
of the seasons draw out the Summer crops.

I have been travelling the rivers of the earth this year
from source to mouth to explain the starred frost
in the night light on your window, the silver paddocks
of lost forest where the moon once moved in black shadows.
There is no one here who can feel the westerly press down
in Autumn, the sheets crack on the line, the empty footstep
in kitchen and bedroom on ice bound mornings.

Alone in a mosquito net, white fall of rain
splashing in bamboo and pine, I think of you
growing like the silkworm into emptiness
wrapped in the self shrouds of mood and language.
In night rains so near the Yangtze tears mean little.
I turn with the sweat of my dreams, throw off the sheet
and try to forget the need to be close to you.

Morning, a bird calls in drips of water.
So far away, days and journeys never come to an end,
sons and fathers never meet at the same river landing
but at dawn on the mid-year turning between ice and heat
I can write as Li Bai did in the kingdom of Wu
to a far country out of love and pain, out of China
where the mulberry fruits and the future lies curled in its cocoon.

(Anhui province, June 1982)

20

Changes

Three "loves" in one line you wrote in August:
by November all was gone, and Spring was done.
Five Springs the garden lasted; more, it must
have changed the country's weather, made it one
sure steady season, instead of drought and rain:
for that's the way we live, risking the unknown,
the changes in the weather, no pleasure without pain,
and growing, only sometimes reap what we have sown.
Five Springs I've loved you, together and apart;
put by the seeds for better seasons, and though
the drought came on, I hoped within my heart
some hidden spring would get us through.
Sometimes the rains don't come, the bore runs salt,
but weather changes, and sweet water finds its way through faults.

from *Confessions of*
a Corinthian

Cut Throat

It hung from the soft wood of the towel rail,
clutching with two claws like the soft leather fruit bat,
but hard and black with its patina of use.

Fit mate for the Solingen razor, the final mystery
hidden away from the children in the cupboard
with its oiled stone, curled in its tortoise-shell.

I was learning the Catechism at the time—
tested in the faith, answering the Canon on my knees
and thinking of that razor as he prayed for me.

Of how you must always lay the razor on the strop,
never at an angle for it cuts hide like butter.
Of how with the stone you must have the proper angle,

push the blade away from you, then use your eye,
subtlest and most vulnerable organ, to test its edge
where the air itself is cut away and ceases to be.

Of how you must hook your finger to lock the blade
and find the grain and cutting angle of your beard,
softened by heat and lather. Then steel, leather and stone

remove the visible and outward signs that prayer
seemed powerless to heal—that nightly growth
which pushed its way into each yielding day.

Bathing Between the Flags

Out of my depth, I'm swimming in the beach
among bare tits: flaccid, upright, pink and brown:
like the shags, the flesh I hunt is where I drown:

bleached sand with streaks of coal and clam
and here and there brown pools Narcissus deep
where self-regarding bodies wax in oily sleep.

Skin wrinkles, burns into prune, tits sag, and bellies flop.
My peers hide under shade, but in the sun stripped to their crotch
young flesh fills out the concaves of eroded rock.

Nothing is new, it's only changed: mothers from daughters,
sand from rock, the shape of breasts, her yellow hair,
they dance and shimmer through the years' distorting air.

But now the world's a rip beyond the flags,
shadows are flying, bags, half-eaten crusts,
flesh and sand scatter before the Southerly gusts.

My head in a towel, I lie between the flags and do not move:
the sun streams down, the beach begins to flow
and fills the eyes and ears of those who strain against its undertow.

Any Port

Mother used to take us out to the beach
through Kennedy's pineapple farm
along the red-dirt road that led to the top of Transit.
She'd have a picnic basket with a fresh white serviette
pick up two pineapples then start at Lighthouse
and work back to town, beach by beach. It'd take all day:
chase the kelp and jump on the slimy air-filled grapes at Miner's,
root through the shingle at Shelly's for slivers of mother-of-pearl,
over the rocks and swing on the needled branches by Nobby's
where the waves set in white and stiff as a Sunday
tablecloth shook out with crumbs of spray and sand--
then we'd cross Twopenny with the dazzle of noon in our eyes
the wind cracking and the sand stinging our legs to the cave under Flagstaff
where mother'd set the cloth and the sandwiches and the pineapple
and the scones Gran'd made and the jam and the relish
and they all tasted of the impatience of salt and sun

which is different from the way beer tastes on Saturday
in the bad light of a winter morning on the tablelands
where the hungry rain lashes the window of the pub
and nobody wants to leave to face the music long after lunch.

The New England Almanac

Too long on the tablelands and you believe
   the world is only fire and ice.
On Anzac Day, the first flame is raised in the grate,
   and the goats are put together in the back paddock.

Melbourne Cup, and not a day before, tomato plants,
   which K-Mart has had for weeks, are orphaned out.
Even then, tea-cosied with pots and newspapers,
   the Grosse Lisse shivers in the frost,

and the farmer's bed still has the leckie blanket
   on, on Christmas Eve—just in case.
Between the festival of sacrifice and the festival of loss,
   tablelands people dream of passionate coasts.

The farmer stretches to the warm rump of his wife
   from the freezing fringe of the Onkaparinka,
and thinks himself floating in New Year at Lake Cathie,
   in a foot deep doona on a cold water-bed.

In his dream he flies the black calendar
   of road, white bars of days disappearing
under the car, the trailer, the tent,
   across plains made lunar by frost,

through superfine acres of bitter brittle grass
   where the sun hangs ready to disappear forever:
across sheep-biting streams and gravel-toothed culverts
   where gorges lurk like wolves in gummy paddocks.

Every fifteen miles he can see houses unsheltered,
    bald as granite, where women married at eighteen
say with wonder 'I grew up with my kids',
    until the cleared land ends and the chthonic journey starts.

Here is the forest and the escarpment, purgatory
    of 173 bends in 55 kilometres,
before the river flats, the open road
    and a clear vision of the sea.

Here he starts back to childhood: warmth,
    wet, and giving cheek, where
sunburn and heatstroke, headaches and sulks
    are forgotten, and the only moan he hears

is that of the westerly when he wakes at three
    with the covers pulled off and his wife
laying claim to more of the bed than the bank.
    A dream between two days, which makes a year.

The NRMA (Nothing Really Matters Any More) Guide

Whether you can go by that road
    or find another in time of flood,
or whether you say bugger it and head
    for the uplands where the water drains rapidly

are decisions made on the spot
    without proper knowledge, but which
say more about you and life (yours)
    than any horoscope or curriculum vitae.

On the way up you drive carefully—
    there are land-slips or rock-slides round
every corner, and the shire bridges
    were never sound, especially after fires,

and even when you reach those
    tableland towns where wind and ice
clean out the dusty passions of the main street
    you can't relax, the roads are open

but they lead nowhere except to each other—
    from stock to station agents, from Imperial
to Federal Hotels, from one shut railway station to another,
    in splendid isolation on heights beyond floods.

So all you can do is go to the Royal
    book a room of cold lino and 40-watt globe for the night
count the years in the rings of the wash-basin
    and ruminate on your lamb and three veg:

here where the last ash should have been shaken into
    the Vat 69 ashtray years before, you lie
thinking about fires and floods on coasts and plains
    while rain drops on the iron roof like hot fat on a grill.

A whole life stretched out on singed chenille
    reading the fine-print of the inn-keeper's act
waiting for the future to break down the door
    from which the last occupant removed the knob.

Luxe, Calme, et Volupté

So I took out the boat and made a difficult shore:
sand, tall pines, a small hill, light breaking in waves
on warm rocks. The nor'-easter laid the hull over,
hissed, slapped round thin wood and brought the beach to me—
wind, water, sand drawn here in one knot;

but there in the thyme's gold and orange there was not
another to be seen, no one waiting on that shore
counting hours, the pale blue star, its phosphor waves,
for the dark sail had cast its pall over
the bronze land stretching to reach me.

Dreams, as much for Baudelaire, Matisse, leach me,
melt through the page, run into oil until the knot
unties, wind and water fly apart, the shore
expands, burns, is quenched by bitter waves,
darkness and gibbets grow, the small hill over-

whelmed by importuning and futility, hell over
runs, until through the black hole, gold reaches to me,
black sides everting into light, the topos a knot
tied into untying, evolving, turning as the shore
sliding into and out of sight under my waves;

but now the bay and headland clears where someone waves—
blue, indigo, yellow scents from porphyry walls over
the sea, the wind warm from the land reaches for me
and the gold burns above a line of hills. It was not
the sea I knew but one I see through you, another shore.

So the boat took me to that difficult shore
to where your six naked bodies lie beside the waves,
and there you let me watch the flower unfold, petal over
petal, each one you, as you run, worry, laze, teaches me
the meaning of my world: you, as you tie your hair up in a knot.

In 'The bar at the Folies-Bergères'

Her eyes have slipped
the barmaid doesn't see the acrobat about to jump
only the blurred dress-circle as her gaze turns in.
The band fades out,
the conversation's gone:
silent and lost, she sleeps within the circus,
her dreams and voices all her own.

But other eyes are watching,
the man in top-hat
sees another harmony and luxury,
he caught the acrobat's green feet
and set the powdered grains of light
upon her mouth and eyes, the bowl of fruit,
and put the flowers and cameo at her breasts.

Behind the girl, within the mirror, is another dream:
the audience conspires and flirts,
the acrobat holds out his hand
the girl leans out to look directly in his eyes,
while she, still lost between her dream and his,
hearing the rattle of the circus drum,
waits to be taken in the middle of her fall.

The Bar at the Rock Garden, Covent Garden, November 1981

It's really the girl behind the bar at the Rock Garden
        Covent Garden
November 1981, this poem is about. Don't believe titles
        they tell you
as much about what's going on as the band:
Batik Beat, The Clash, Under the Last Arch, The Flats,
        they're the ones
I've come to hear, love, yes, you there, with your sharp
        hair highlighted
in blonde with black velvet band, black top to match
        around drooby
comfortable tits, off-white trousers creased around
        pendicular arse
a blind white face smooth as the Guinness she's pouring
        and as much head—
remember Manet in 1881 seeing another girl with black
        velvet choker
eyes and face vacant as the mirror behind her—here tonight
        behind her
the band beats out double time, some reggae, like a
        Turkish steel band
and the men pose in their agony wrapping their mouths
        around a blind
microphone, blasting the black paint off soft gut walls
        saying I am
male male male male, but no one hears them over the
        simple beat, not you
pressing a button for a measured pint—it fills the glass
        to the very top
black with a cream head, loud music in a small room,
        overflowing.

A Sum Over Histories

i.m. Richard Feynman and A. D. Hope

Drawn from the die of the great zero of being
along the straight plumb line of becoming,
our hero makes his quest at forty-five degrees
up the slope between life's x and y axes.

There the co-ordinates of ante and post quo—
A and B: the path between, a slow
and upward grind against a killing gradient;
he leaps the crumbling mid-point to the present salient.

Counting his steps, he takes stock at this station
on the painful way, notes the equation
of length and angle, despairs at the bodkin in his hand
and presses on to B against the running sand.

Here let us stop like Donne's great prince in prison,
or Bunyan in his cell, in indecision:
the body leads one way, the righteous soul the other,
two eyes on space, on time the inner other.

Heisenberg could hopscotch from point to point in play,
others see thorny turnpikes as the way.
The poet chooses his own vademecum, the world
if there is time enough, then time to make his world:

thrusting out of the yawning O, the black abyss,
the angel y of time, and our nemesis
the earthward sideways slide of the serpent x of space.
He writes, plots A and B with metaphor, a date, a place,

A known, B yet to come. But the road, the signs?
Like Donne's flat map our life lines
stretch across the deserts and the flood plains of our palms
doused in sweats and dry in fever, calendars of harms.

In sinuosities, meanders, anabranches, in arrows and in leaps,
 time makes its world lines across the deep;
probable connections, trajectories, parabolas proliferate
until their interfering patterns cancel all but the immediate.

These are the sums of all our histories combined,
the integral path of body and the mind,
a prison cell in Bedford, a coffin for a chastened bed,
the soul's last flight, and the great gates opening ahead.

Suburban Sonnet

after Gwen Harwood

The smell of Cold Power on your typing fingers,
avoiding bed, a poem while the children sleep.
A sink of washing; bad temper lingers
like chip fat round the stove: you curse, they weep.
Critical glances at a lack of buttons,
creases and burns, felted hair, tch tch they cluck—
the lone male with his brood, so gossip gluttons,
hovers, picks every grain, counts every fuck.
It was an accident the milk was spilt:
his drinking, her career, life in the dregs.
Her sisters told her that there was no guilt
it's just another nest with china eggs.
A dirty trick like all the others:
to turn free women into suburban mothers.

For Gwen

Bugger the milk, it was the ink we spilt which mattered.
Instead of blood running down the stairs, a dribble of words,
God's little lamb, not the baby, which was battered
Every time we looked for sacraments in nappy turds.

Solace, the nightly biro used to fight depression,
To catch the galvanising cries of the newly born—
Ideas which need the night to fix their impression
On the daily grind of making bread from alien corn.

But now they have grown to beards and periods, pregnancies
And being at the birth—knee-deep in life's umbles
There is no need to worry of their failure to thrive.
That nagging cot-death cry which broke our fancies
Still persists, we use it when the muse stumbles
To heat the cooling bottle. *We* have eaten them alive.

Ubi Sunt?

'A place for everything and everything in its place!'

The timber wharf, the oil wharf, the silo—
Alec and I did the rounds every morning,
my first job in the world of men.

The Dolphins, Lee Wharf, King's Wharf,
then back to the Dyke, the Electrics,
then the sixty-milers at the Hydraulics.

What was in? The *Canopus*, the *William MacArthur*,
or the *Birchgrove Park*? *Canopus* with the cast-iron plates
ochred in red-lead and carbuncular with rivets

which rusted while her plates stayed smooth
as the tally-man's fob-watch. *Canopus* of the aft-end stack,
the stylish transom, yet ten years a wreck on a Kiwi coast;

her age, a year for every mile she butted through
to White Bay to give the big smoke its neons and its lights—
Canopus at the hydraulics loading coal must still be there.

The wagons ghost down the bank: Ayrfield,
Bellbird, Stockrington, Pelton Main
one by one they're swung up by the crane

dowager-skirted, bob-weighted
an angry Tenniel queen put to work
in a steel and steam wonderland, she picks

at the rake—the wagon hangs like a beast
while the pinboss swings his sledge,
the bottom opens and a rush of coal

I hear it seconds—now years—later—bang
hiss of dust and the sigh of the ship
as she settles under the weight of the past.

In the dark chaos of the hold the coal trimmer
makes mesas from the coal's volcanic cones—
his drilled shovel shapes unseen order—

I see it later in the afternoon
in the spirit-level plimsoll touching the water's face,
in her blue-peter set flying high in the gale.

A pitching vessel full of hearth-light and fire,
the embalmed smell of bacon cooking, and steam,
—white as a pudding cloth—from the donkey engine,

she sinks belly-deep into the swell, turning south
into the liquid present, a slinking, fawning bitch,
squirming across her master's moods;

this is *Canopus* set for Sydney past Barrenjoey,
where the *Birchie* foundered in a squall
her hatches open to a whelming sea;

Canopus riding the sharp pie-crust light
of summer morning waves, or the corrugated
grey-blue troughs skillioning in from winter south;

Canopus full of soft condensing steam,
cabbage water, oily rag-waste, salt dungarees,
now a cold winking word set far away

beyond the timber wharf, the silo,
the Dolphins, Lee Wharf, King's Wharf—
I call her name to the oil and dunnage of these empty berths.

Mann's Bookshop

I've lost the place now in the changes:
there was a hole-in-the-wall pub one side,
and on the other, Jo-Anne's Frock Salon.

Inside, a Gothic nave buttressed with books—
some valuable, lots that weren't, and Jim
(Newell to his wife) in constant traffic

from the till to the next door bar,
leaving me to mind the mysteries:
darkness, books, ideas, strange people

where I spent hours after school
getting an education, learning the language
of non-conformity and wit.

The deal counter with zinc edges,
a grubby window, soot from Civic,
a green enamelled door, red letters—

there's no sign of them in Hunter Street.
A concrete pavement, the hard refractive
surfaces of glass throw back the summer light.

But the dark of books, the hidden truths
behind the light we're taught and forced to know
are always there if we can find the door,

not in this street, but in my head:
my mind, Jim Mann's bookshop,
my art, his window with my letters on it.

Caveat Emptor

'This is the Victor Ice Cream Show,
We're on the air from 2KO.
We're brought to you by Victor,
The name you know so well;
You eat the bloody packet
And you chuck the rest to Hell.'

Rationing ended and in 1950 consumers were born.
I was nine at the time, shifty and nervous, a pawn
to the big girls' queens: I did what I was told.
'We're taking you to the show at 2KO.'
O.K. I ate my ice-cream-so cold it broke the spoons—
sat in stunned silence at Uncle Rex's jokes,
and sang along with Auntie Hazel's transparent tunes.

'The Yellow Rose of Texas' and 'Peter Cottontail'
we croaked, craning our necks as male and female
tried to see who was where: I liked the blonde
from Berner Street, in sixth class, one of the elite;
and when I'd dare I'd wander past her place
wondering what magic was locked fast
within those walls: to find the gateway through a pretty face.

Even through the door, I find the face is what I remember.
You, blue eyes dilated, black cores of surrender
stare up at me as I enter at the gate, yet
the path obstinately remains my own; always I come home.
There is no liquid centre to the chocolate, the lamb lacks mint—
hasty consumer of the party's prizes, now my tongue is numb
with cold, and your kisses have a taste of paper and of print.

from *Ocean Island*

Industrial Waste

Muck and money

A collar lasted a day
by night black-ringed
it matched your cuffs
carried its tithe of soot
from the smoke fall
of Zaara St powerhouse
tugs, steam rollers, winter fires
the school train
and the Leviathan itself
the Works
casting shadows into the city

red when the ore came in
bucketed out into the westerly
a slipstream of Iron Knob
across Stockton's washing

and black from smelting and refining fires
burning away all night
the iron's maculations
which found their way by day
into the armpits of our shirts
and gave the tincture to our hands
of others' labours and their sins

there were compensations:
they told us in this world
as part of Adam's contract
'where there's muck there's money'
so you got on your bike
and went to work, and got on

your bike and came home
glad of your pay packet's
solid billet in your pocket

but when the ash-pit finally cools
the coke ovens are quenched
and the last arterial stream of iron runs into sand,
the covenant of soot will be broken
the grimy cuffs removed
and the lucid air
of the old faith will cover the city,
and from Smelter's Beach the heath
will bloom with honey flowers
the bell miner sound the hours
around the abandoned pit
and the secret bush reclaim
the refractories and kilns

then with the harrowing
of this century, this millennium,
the dark mills grind up their own,
fresh fields return
and the three watches of the day
sleep the one shift of night

and when the smoke lifts
what will we be then?

Cottage industry

Where the lime-burners fired
the previous owners' middens

where casked water was floated
over a river of thirst to the town

where the worst and the rejected
ended up in mangroved exile

there are the sea pits and a new town—
pubs, slips, boat houses, a ferry—

and behind it the poppet-heads of wealth
spinning-wheels unravelling a seam

deep in the earth, plying from below the sea
a string of wagons full of vanished swamp

high onto the bright morning wharves,
old ironbark trunks and planks fringed

with a reed bank of masts, flags in flower,
furred seed heads of furled spars:

waiting for a tide to Chile. A strange harvest
which never failed, until the tide turned

and mud flats, oily and labile, were pumped
from deserts into the new asphalt cities of the car.

Labour and Capital

I worked with a man who could hardly breathe:
a chest like a forty-four gallon drum,
shoulders three pick-handles across.

Used to being a big man his voice was now two sizes too small,
and his body hung like a droughty scarecrow's—
they had put him in charge of the sweepers.

He told me. Wheezing. Coughing. Eyes watering
like it was the first morning smoke. About relining
the blast furnace with high temperature bricks.

Good news for the share-holders, down-time
got less and less (a pause for air) as the boss
found ways of getting back into the furnace sooner.

Two sugar bags, fore and aft, dripping wet,
a steaming sandwich-board
as soon as you stepped in the oven,

your breath cooled from dry lime-kiln white
into scalding fog. He hawked the memory from his lungs.
And then you laid red-hot bricks with leather gloves.

The smell of burning hide as you picked out bricks
told you what your feet knew through your boots,
this is what sunday school had promised,

and now you were in it even though you hadn't
broken any commandment except covet
your neighbour's new fridge and car:

five minutes before you were relieved,
though that went up to seven when
the credit squeeze was on, and ten off,

for four hours, then a break, and back
into it, week after week, all through
the prosperous 'fifties when all was well.

Old metals

Copper, colour of the goddess herself, Venus.
Iron, so old its origins are in war.
And Tin, metal of the underworld.

Their alloys and amalgams, shaping and bright,
worked into knots and laminations,
edged and pointed to logic's limits,

or poured into patterns of the flower and star,
threaded, screwed, filed, turned, fitted
into the set of mind's geometry,

the tools of old metals are early poems:
made from the gods, they left their mark
to butcher, carve, build, and kill.

Oil wharf

a set of dolphins each with its oil point
and the storage tanks beyond the road
brilliant white in a landscape of grease and soot

the oil came sliding in in neat post-war tankers
flying the winner's bunting, ESSO, Shell, Caltex,
and out through petrol palaces in the suburbs

the wharf strangely was clean,
the bollards seagull white,
the strainers whole and unsplit,

but underneath, and out of sight,
oil spread its deadly rainbow
over a dark and silent sky

Silos

Had someone dropped a bomb?
There was never anyone there:

a necropolis of bone-white tombs
columbaria for germ that will never seed
perfect marble cylinders topped
with corrugated iron sheds
an Australian Parthenon

they wait for two weeks every year
the golden wave at Christmas
that sweeps down from the plains
and the dusty evacuation
of autumn's Anzac day

between them someone fishes
and a boy moons in the long shadows
of a cold war's winter's sun.

Dyke End

the men come on at seven-thirty
pinboss, coal-trimmers, shunters
and king of all, the crane man

a ship is under the electrics
like a patient under a doctor
wide open, vulnerable, cure or kill

and the operation starts
the trussed wagon slung over the gaping belly
the sledge smashed on the hinge-bolt's head

and the terrible gasp and collapse of coal
blackened souls tumbling back into chaos
a ruined forest smoothed by minor devils

as the ship sinks deeper and the crane crows
the men blacken and fill the farthest corners
with their work to the spirit level of the sea

the shift comes off at four, the hammer,
shovel, rope and sling put up, and full
of the nightmare, she waits for the tide

Timber wharf

It takes twenty minutes to walk there:
up the high-level bridge across the shunting lines,
down, across the dockyard tracks, to the wharves

and up river half a mile: an intricate path and dangerous,
to find when you get there that yesterday the *Waipiri*
out from the islands has left a grove of sandalwood on the wharf.

You can smell it as soon as the river breeze gets behind it:
walking west towards the red dust cliffs of the works
above creosote and hydraulic oil you know there is

another world: you track through it for half a mile
until you reach the sawn bound billets of bleeding logs
stepped like ghats at the river side, pyres of perfume

smoking entrails of forests plucked out and thrown here
to dislocate the mind through false scents.
Twenty minutes, and a lifetime to find the way back.

The oyster bank

Were there really oysters there?

or did some ironic tar name it that
for the ribbed and bearded hulls ripped open
no matter whether wood or iron,
whatever ship that wandered there

blown from the grasp of nursemaid tugs
running free down the roads outside the harbour
bang on to the drowned flats
sluiced from farms and gullies miles away.

Oysters need tides and food,
twice daily baptisms and communions,
was the water shallow enough?
it is now: a breakwater of wrecks

made from disasters of air and water
cemented into place so no storm will move them
and a safe Sunday walk into the elements
but not an oyster anywhere.

Floating dock

an old freighter in dock
bare hull humped up
to show its shameless secret places
birth-naked and stranded-
screw, rudder, bearded bilges,
blunt cut-water, toothless transom-
age should be clothed

not penned in a steel change room
propped up and told not to move
while air and steam drain you
of all that holds you on an even keel
high and dry as workers paint you up
with the useful crimson of anti-foul

vital signs are still there, the stack smokes
lights glitter in fo'c'stle and poop
incontinent waters vent, and on the halyards
flags still proclaim name and purpose,
not yet paid-off and headed for the breaker's yard

but nothing signs from the floating dock
grey in its war-time camouflage it is the sea
bearing up on steel waves its cousin ships—
amphibian of time and change it sinks and rises
to its own tides, but carries no flag of its own

Phosphate wharf

just a hopper and some trucks
and a bucket grab bringing up white dirt
from inside the best-looking ship in the harbour

a clipper bow, sleek lines and cut-away counter
the *Cutty Sark* with funnels
this is exotic *Triona*, ex Ocean Island

her bow-sprit sheaves set moorings
off harbour-less phosphate islands
deep in a boy's imagined Pacific

tiny jewels along the equator
they glow in a pre-dawn bedroom
necklaced along the fibro ceiling

sometimes green on rose, or french blue on white
the surf grumbles on flower bed reefs
the lagoon trembles with an indigo wind

full of possibilities, like a new day,
but here the surf is oceanic and the beach
like concrete, and school a brick prison

where when the nor-easter sets in
a thin dribble of white dust reaches the playground
and the dream top-dresses Wickham's bitumen

Chrome works

This is as close to alchemy
as tradesmen get
the hard bright currency
on base moulds of perfect shapes
migrating metals to other poles
like a world transposed
in an etching's negative
to the positive of print

Dark shop where all is touched by acid
curtains are cobwebs, walls furred
with salts and oxides
the concentrate of industry is here
nothing made but changed
by dark illuminations
of paradise on metal plates

Dockyard

Mother's sewing room but run by men.

Filthy with rust and dust, steel fabric is cut
by flaming scissors; sparks, blobs of hot metal
glue the gusseted bits, and seams of rivet pins
run round the paunch of the belted keelson,

and over there is a mangle bending
crusted sheets, wringing the last drop out
before the steel sets into complex curves
hung out to dry on a bony bush of ribs.

Dark and dirt, mazes with red-lead hedges,
companionways and three-storey heights
inside the nave of the engine room,
sphinctered hoses, chalked graffiti: mother

is another world, of ticking treadle,
damp comfort of a hissing pot,
the lavender gloom of linen presses,
a footfall in the hallways of sleep

away from the suck of poppet valves,
the stamp of steam hammers, the stink
of flux and electric arcs, somewhere
beyond the slipway where in months

this inert metal with its fields of force,
steam, fire, oil, water, the womb of men,
will slide into its proper world,
launched at last into that other sex.

After a war (any war)

In Freetown I sat by the radio for two years
listening to the short wave
roll back and forth across Biafra:

Ikot Ekpenni, Owerri, Port Harcourt
—just down the coast—while I watched,
safe, above the harbour, as the sun set

deep in the slavers' Atlantic.
So far above it all—and beyond
what happened in Long Tan

or Mi Lai. Out of that because I
was conceived when my father
was on leave in September 1940

and born when he was on manoeuvres
five months before he went to Malaya
and three and half years as a prisoner.

Safe in the peace of existential depression—
the in-grown anxiety of life of those
who were in school when the Yalu River

burst, and never had to face the Chinese
human wave which swept the next generation
of diggers back to Panmunjon;

and safe in the hothouse hedonism
of booze and travel on the right side
of the iron curtain, I warmed myself

by the cold war's electric tension,
stretched to the thrill of militant peace
and marched in moratoriums,

until I sit here in Merewether and watch the sun come up
from Chile and Argentina and their dirty wars
and shine on me now at the water's edge

an open beach far from the harbour I once called home
where the dead and mutilated were stacked
in stinking piles in Wilberforce last January:

I saw the photos and the news as it happened
on the net, before the sun which curdled those corpses
arrived to warm this open beach

where in 1942 they thought the Japanese would land
and we were evacuated for three months until
that horror passed, and even now I wake

in the night and hear the planes come in
and the tidal wave of swamping change
rise out of usual horizon and bear us all away

to today where the westerly has laid everything flat
and the surf slides and creeps like history
and someone listens for signal in all the noise

                    *

and that noise is now
the present confused with all its freight
of what has gone before—different for each of us

the noise of spring and freesias in the lawn
the first butterflies and we were on the beach:
swimming before breakfast

the water cold as the wave which drops
from the opened ice-chest
but the top layer of sand dried like old mortar

warm to walk on but frangible and breaking
through into the cold underworld
which our feet are always part of

poised to take their first plunge of the year,
father and son, into the antarctic current
to be chilled into sudden salty life

my father who made such ingenious things
as my own life and now his again
in this new world of peace

who locked up the slavering human beast of war
in a peace-time house and garden
with tennis court and surf laid on

it seemed proof against anything, and as I
float in the cold current of the rest of my life
always within coo-ee of the beach

he rises in the morning wind toward our new dawn
and disappears forever into the fiery
eye of the beast he thought he had finally tamed

     *

a death by fire makes minor headlines
though it happens every day in lesser ways
and there is his in the sydney morning herald

but the obsequies which followed in our
industrial town were of a fitting nature
ash in the grate, gritty smoke in every eye

nothing is made without fire
and nothing undone without its virtue
so everywhere had fire

tiled and domesticated in its cast iron
basket it warms the house-bound
and is the child's vision of the world to come

more alive than the sleeping dog it is book
and song and sunlight, comforting nurse
without big sister's smoke and smell

the backyard incinerator which consumes
all that is dead and past, or uncle's open hearth
where fallen angels play with magic pokers

to create the new, or mother's gas ring
grandma's copper, close relatives in steam
with all that graze along the wharves and railway lines;

bright fire is story and belief in mysteries,
so when they told me you were a box of ashes
it seemed that was how things were each cold morning

a new start with the broom and pan, clear out the past,
put it in a box, and post it in a wall
along a garden where roses grow, clean, equal and confined

like an equation which explains the world
that though the outer shells may change
within life's energies are always conserved

perhaps that's why I've never returned
to see if the roses grow, especially 'Peace'
the one they'd just released the year before

and if the wall is standing, the long honey-comb
of bricks grouted together by so many bodies,
not to weep upon but to stare at and realise

that everything is still the way it was
and nothing changed, though I am older
now than your own father when you died

nor have I brought my sons to see the fruits of peace
blooming in vigorous display among their thorns
because, thank god, they have yet to know a war

                    *

so all my life, though I have been to none,
I have carried within me a war, and scars,
like a birthmark without cause or pride

invisible stains of peace from when men came
home to that other world of women and found
that neither recognised the other, unfamiliars

who spoke different languages and lived different lives,
two hemispheres in one household where each
inhabits other seasons and reads other skies at night,

tribes of children who do not know their fathers
and resent the stranger ignorant of their rituals,
hard men whose eyes are blank as Caesar's as they watch

for faults, then walk down sleepless moonlit corridors
in search of the peace they waited for so long—
who find it here, in my own wakenings in the night,

when in the dark of all those years I hear at last
the sounds of parents talking—it is the white noise
of peace: the sleeping babble of the kids at night.

Newcastle, 2000

Marking Time

for Jane and Felicity

I had an office once
with a window and a calendar.
I spent more time looking out
the calendar than the window.
Every morning I marked off
another day, eager to get to
where?
   I left the office,
as you leave everywhere in the end,
and found another window
to match the butcher's calendar,
marking time until I got to here

and remembered what butchers always knew,
that marking lambs and pigs
with rubber band or knife
will make them grow and lose the taint
which comes with time—
but robs them of their future hopes.

I've marked too many essays,
castrated too many days,
it's time to spend what I've been spared.

Dragons

for Bobby

There must be a deep need for them
for although Nature in all her experiments
never got round to dragons,
there they are:

winged like fruit bats, serpent-scaled,
cats'-eyed, owl-wise,
and talking in parrot-tongues,
but most of all imbued with human breath
capable of razing forests,
turning ice mountains to melt-water
and making deserts from ungulate savannahs.

They are us:
virgin hungry,
solitary but necessarily social,
full of mysterious destiny,
but never fully in control.

They are our other:
extinct, before they're born.

Late autumn days

Might the Almighty have chosen
late harvest grapes for his aperitif
while He watched our Parents
sleep dreamlessly in unpruned orchards?

Idleness, bliss, each sweet sticky hour
as they sleep on,
unaware, uncomprehending
of who they are, consanguine
with all those whom Adam named
once his missing rib untied his tongue.

Let them sleep in vineyards
only gods can enjoy.
The time will come when
calloused fingers, sunburnt heads
will be the medals of great vintages

Baths

wire netting kept the sharks out
but it didn't keep the kids in

the catwalk boards to the final pile
were like live coals to wet feet
barge and belt until someone
went off over the side into the real world

out there with the grey nurse
and the blue-ringed octopus.
where future horrors were present
laughter, king of the cat walk

walking his planks jumping on
urgent fingers trying to get back
on to the slippery slope inside
the cage, chicken-wire heroes

the baths were houses
built with water, extensions of school,
flooded suburbs, white australia,
swimming within the margins of terror

from *After a War*
(any war)

Fishing for Meaning

You make things in your life—
in my case only for meaning not for use.
You wonder who'll find them in the back shed
after you're ashes on the mantelpiece,
and what sense they'll make of them.
Like those wagons scuttled down in the gully
beyond the pit, tangled in lantana.
I saw only wheels sunk in clay,
chains rotten with rust,
and teak drawbars with surgical lumps out of them.
At a garage sale last week I found
a fishing reel, its dense wood taking
a shine from a patina of oil
full of the flickering light of winter nights
while someone worked carefully dreaming
of summer flathead by burning coals.

table mountain

you wouldn't know it was there
hiding behind drawn white fogs
until someone needed to see out
then in a wind shift
the city has another dimension
sheer sides and flat falls
the taciturn oldest resident
hangs over back fences
saying he won't be moved
and all day every day
he's there, grand in his looming presence
until the city retreats into its white
sea mist, dreaming it's still at sea
and never made this landfall
safe in transit with no address
and no need to break bread
at the common table

Tide Line

the moon's breath got to here and left
a scribble of dunnage, a line
of found objects, which mark

where the sky's ribs arched
and let go to rest, sank
back at peace and left its poems

for me to read walking the margin
between work and rest, that point
when we will move our house like crabs

to an empty shell cast up by change
and fitting like a glove, or your love,
to use an easy but difficult word

which just chimes in, like the sound
of your breath as you sleep beside me,
curled up like the sound of the sea

Time and Motion

Family Photos

Kootingal Platform, April 2011

a family waits
waits for a train or a photograph
formally posed for the moment to happen

it could be 1911
bags packed for the Royal Show
the father four years from Anzac Cove

it could be 1941
kit bag slung over the back
wife and kids hanging on to the last

or even 1971
first prize in the ballot
and a bullet in Da Nang waiting

the train arrives and departs
no one aware of what comes next
heaving themselves on board

surrendering their will
to the ringing grooves
of this cursed century

borne on to this moment
as the train glides out
from autumn to winter

uneasy fingers checking
for a ticket's reassurance
a place, a date, and the promise of return

The dying fire (in mid-winter)

for my grand-son

The great log I put on just after tea
is now black char—
bright ruby coals beneath,
above a honeycomb of tar.

The room is warm, still full of life
that's now tucked up in bed,
his noise an after-glow of light
around his blanket-shrouded head.

The red gum's dismembered limbs
lie waiting for tomorrow's funeral pyre,
which once in spring-time winds
waved to the sun to catch its fire.

They'll live again as debts returned.
I switch out the lights. The grate's still warm
from a September sun which burned
before my son was born.

buoy

a life is an unbounded field,
an ocean not a lake,
open-ended until the very end,
it's self-organising
always capable of revision and correction

when it has an end, like any story,
it ends up in the hands of others
and then another boundary is made,
futile, because it is a set within a set,
infinite in its recursive meanings

as eager children search in your bottom drawer
for clues—some permanent point
from which to make their sense
of who they are, where they came from

an iron stake is driven into the ocean of life
which once was you

that day when the three of us
drifting back from a day's outing on the sloop
turned into the wind and I went for'ard
with the boat-hook to pick up the buoy

which my grandfather had laid fifty years before

domain

I've sold their house—
disbursed their furniture and pretty things
with the abandon of a drunken earl

the empty floors echo a new vista
the last ten or fifteen years of my life
will be an open door, an empty garage

so, walk into that strange street
without the elastic band
of returning home or seeing them again

it's the freedom of vacant possession

1980 — Post-War Retrospective

Mushrooms, Early 1946

Yellow light from the car headlights pales
as we swing east across the flats to where
the sand piles and breaks slowly west

cow paddocks under the loom of grey dawn
mortise fence   paper bark   a windmill creaking
the smell of byres and swamps, cow pats steam

I have climbed through the fence
chased through the wetness
steam-brown and black like the dog in his kennel

to pearl silver tops, new worlds of dawn sky
beneath, trenches of velvet brown

I tear them from the ground
throw them in the billy
more more more ... I tire ... too many

and dad? I stop
the car door is open and he is half out
staring at me

all this time

"Newcastle from Memorial Drive, 1947"

Howard Ashton, Newcastle Art Gallery

In the Ford's chrome and bakelite
over the Hill to your Mother's
we pass a man at an easel
painting the empty blue of the Basin
its silo and the thin ribs of smoke
from Port Waratah.

And there are the clouds
from last night's rain, Nesca's pond,
the Dyke, and North Arm's waste of water
crooked as the track you took me home on ...

I am left behind

the black Mercury rolls on,
I can see through the oval window the back of your head;
in the glove-box coupons; there is a scar on your left hand;
the torn stitching in the back seat;
broken brass couplings from the hoses;

it turns into High Street and disappears.

I am alone in the gallery
waiting in these concrete and synthetic fastnesses
for the car to come back,
but it doesn't

I stare hard, there, at centre of the picture
where under the red-tiled roof in Nesca Parade
you and grandmother must now be drinking tea

the man folds up his easel
packs away those years ago
this hole in the wall
which opened like an awful wound
the moment I walked in here

Hail Storm, New Year, 1947

not only the iceman brings ice in summer:

winds smell of undersea
a bruise darkens the sky
it's the end of the world at the start of the year

on the beach kids run from a rolling wave of air
inside there is a knocking and hammering on frosted glass
water bubbles mouth at the shrunken frame
'come in ... come in ...'

darkness is first footing this family with white coal
it grins pearls of melting teeth

it's an old friend to dad listening
in the back room sick with malaria

—leave your father alone—chills, sweats,
night curses cloud the day
indelible cancels on rationed sweetnesses

—be quiet your father's sick—
a white world of numb tastes
the day's promises suspended

it's not only the iceman who brings ice in summer

Saturday, early 1948

THIS VESSEL SAILS AT:

FOR:

now many times since
have I chalked in the gaps?

the first time I saw it
it was real enough:

12 noon 14/3/48
Ocean Island

the chalk was, not the island

yet on that hot day: a slight nor-easter, breakfast time
powdered rock tails across the wharf into Wickham
gets in my eyes, smarts as I climb the gang-plank
fret by fret past blue hull, clipper bow, and tucked stern
to the ringing deck, through running eyes I see
the island rising green out of blue
a small beach in a ring of surf
and I feel hungry for it,
clean and bright
the cramp in my stomach
the taste of iron on my tongue
for green trees and chasing into clear water
digging in the sand together you and I
on that beach this ship travels to.

Later, while you listen to the races on the couch
and the others sleep

with nothing to do
I start to remember for the first time,
eyes and bitterness,
and to draw on the back step with a stone
destinations for myself alone

The Track

it's a moonlit night and I'm walking with Dad
God knows where
but down a track
sleepers and rails a ladder to the moon

tall fennel, a yellow flower open to the night
oil on the long-dead rungs of plains trees
the track between two houses
two worlds, two grandmothers

dad? no words, step after step,
did I hold your hand?
I stepped out your footprints
invisible on the clinker ballast
except on the dull gleam of wet sand,

at a level crossing I caught your heavy tread for a moment
then lost it behind the woolshed,
in the empty shelter-sheds at the park and beach,
through the paspalum, behind the tennis courts.
then the bowling club, the cliff, the lane, then home—
where were you?

somewhere ahead but out of sight—

I've followed the crunch of stone
the stirring of long grass
the creak of sand
the moonlight rails
to the light at home
for many years

climbing after you rung by rung

November 1948, November 1980

this is the hard one

what voice to use: the kid's or mine?
is there a difference?

it's two a.m. in the new house
a two-week-old bedroom with a blue light,
some white light from the street-lamp
a world-war-one painting of the desert on the wall
smell of new paint and Masonite

it's time

The Art of War

the visitor

"Afternoon Collaroy – 1940": Adrian Feint*

I've let myself in
he's half expecting me
she's not
nineteen newly-wed and full of life

they're on the beach
he's got a towel and eye out for the sharks
while she's impulsively let everything drop
the hat, the towel, the robe

the on-shore breeze is strengthening
the banksias stir, their sabre leaves
twitch in the morning sun,
blossom hides the hand grenade of seed

he likes his garden this Artist who
could not have a tree without a dove
to coo outside the window
where they spent the morning making love

but now it's noon and all hangs in the balance
and I wait, time means nothing to me now,
and soon he'll move, she'll cling to him,
while all the while his uniform hangs in the dark.

* Cover Image

the morning after

"Coventry Cathedral – 1940": John Piper

those broken slabs of colour were waiting
in november slanting light
the morning after the nighttime raid

a cubist composition of total war
a hint of what all of us were in for
right up to a two dimensional

Hiroshima, end plate of this album
put away among all the others:
frozen history, the rubble

of medieval stone, Christian
Europe eating its own,
Asia poisoned, the world convulsed

until the holy light of the atom
irreducible ultimate
sucked all colour from creation

but on that cold morning
propped on still hot saints
infernal smoke in the nose

someone saw beauty in light
and stone and the ordinary business
of cleaning up the mess

and getting on to tomorrow

the new apocalypse

'"Shelterers in the Tube – 1941": Henry Moore

the colours of judgement day
are black and white
wrapped in grey earth we lie and wait

above, the busy din of angels:
the wailing siren, the crump
and shake of heavenly wrath

it's time to hide pull close the covers
and will the flickering light of life
to stay alight for one more mortal moment

before the earth will part
and we will be sucked upward
in pillars of transforming flame

to face the awful truth
that it is not God nor Beëlzebub
nor frightful Moloch

who consumes us in the fiery furnace
but our neighbor and ourselves
the black and white of rage and love

perspective

"Vernal Equinox – 1943": Paul Nash

the hill   the tree   the moon
of such things
is the world composed

spring in the middle
of that war which gave me life
and took so many others

a place   a time
the rigid geometry
of all compositions

vanishing points
of sentences
the hill   the tree   the moon

setting the scene

"Human Laundry – Belsen 1945": Doris Zinkeisen

the dead and near dead are being washed
laid out on cots in converted stables
bleached skin and bones groomed

by well-fed guards in butchers' aprons
this is the post-war world
the sudden shift from abattoir to hospice

how did she make sense of this?
one week the smell of burning flesh
the next carbolic and rice gruel

pre war she designed for noël and gertie
dressed mannequins and sketched lalique
and then the curtain dropped, scene change

and here we are as the players pack up
the tragedy complete, the dead carried off
the audience sent home to lick their wounds

and on the washing lines across five continents
soiled sheets will flap in cleansing winds
and shrouds wrap lovers in a sun-struck world

war artist

"Nuremburg Trial – January 1946": Laura Knight

'the ordinariness of evil' – don't you believe it:
'unser Hermann' sits opposite me,
his enormous head wobbles, the grin

waxes and wanes like the tide, his
eyes sparkle, he jokes, and nudges,
then falls into a dark mood – he is

the weather we've been sheltering from
these six long years, cyclonic egos
who have unhoused and killed millions

it's hard to be dispassionate, that chin,
like a tyrol rock shelf, the sleek seal skin,
how they filled Speer's arc-lit spaces

no different from Ingres' Napoleon, or
busts of Caesar or Hadrian, the ego
celebrated, the petty man obliterated

but here that day I saw it all, even down
to the fountain pen in his bank manager's suit
which hid the cyanide signature on his great work

the leader

"Winston Churchill – 1954": Graham Sutherland

the war is nine years gone, and after seven
years of famine, call it 'rationing', and seven
years of 'never having it so good' to come

Pharaoh sits on his commoner's throne,
rotund in plenty, still glorying in triumph
over his teetotal, vegetarian antithesis

he is Empire in an age of existential doubt
Victorian certainty in a ruined Europe
ruthless to protect decency and law

his purpose to keep the scepter in its isle
and this above all – to be victor
and write the history of his times

no wonder he thought this portrait 'filthy'—
its after-the-war-to-end-all-wars modernism
shows true colours seeping through a public varnish

and in that bull-dog certainty one can see
doubt, the scars of 1945's rejection
and the scowl and defiance that anyone else

should make a likeness

Orpheus

Underworld, Orphic Meditations

The future behind us

is the lava scar on the island's flank
Pompeii's frozen lovers
Archeopteryx pressed in mud

it is the ship's wake,
dissolving as we watch
the horizon swallow home

the white-out of cloud
as we leave the earth
on the return journey

the dawn chorus of disjointed notes,
dreams to roll over and return to,
the cell's interrogating light

it's our sense of purpose
turned inward into loss,
the paralysis of regret

the sound, the sight of all we loved,
the expectation, the joy, the bliss
that drove the poet to look back

Hades

cool shadows
somnolent quiet
a poppy stroke
of summer heat

curtained dark
of low voices
murmur of all who
hide from noon's inquisition

the kitchen fire is out
the women wait and fan themselves
the old man snores
his consort in her flowered shift
sleeps through the long verandah
of the afternoon

safe in their retreat
refuge against the light
the flaming sword
of a cruel testing land
we shelter deep in
their anagram of shade

Emoh Ruo

feeling my way
along the cedar panelling
at the end of the corridor
the pier glass reflects
the brown carpet progress
from the front door
down the incline towards
the kitchen and the jakes

turn round and there
beside the bedroom door
is a likeness of you
aged seventeen caught
in an oval wooden frame
hand-tinted and signed
by the shire photographer

eyes shut I see
my back in the mirror
know the photograph off by heart
they live in the chthonic dark
of sleep and memory
and I am here to pick you up
take you with me and make again
the world we once shared

if I could find the words
and hear once more the music
of our thoughts, that wind which stirs
along this grim corridor
and promises something beyond
that bolted door—

I feel you touch my arm,
and hear that anxious cough,
and then your voice, and looking
knew it was gone forever.

Taming Tigers

So the poet is like Rilke's panther,
Blake's tiger, Samson's lion,
Dickinson's leopard,
Hughes's jaguar.
It's a zoo in here.

Strike the lyre
Open the cage
Let the mountains roll
The trees dance
The rocks rock

All is transformed
By speech and music
Made whole and harmonious
An order without bars
Changing but the same

So Orpheus found Hell
And charmed its appetite
Made death new life
Found the way out
But couldn't resist

One long last glance at his best work

Aeneid Book VI

The other night I didn't visit the Underworld—
it came to me. My father, not dressed in armour,
or trailing Lethean fogs, but shapeless, formless,
just a feeling, but real, nevertheless,
for loss is an absence, and can only be felt not touched.
And anyway it's so long since I last saw him,
or knew his bodily shape, almost seventy years,
I have no memory of it. But there is a presence:
the one I had in dreams for years after he died—
miraculous returns beside my bed,
the sense of all complete, resolved, the circle squared—
that was the feeling then, and now. But
life is not completion, always open-ended,
a set that's never closed, infinite, recursive,
it takes you by the hand and drags you on,
head turned back over your shoulder,
the elastic touch of memory stretching behind you
back to the Groves of Bliss, the feeling
that all was closed and tucked in tight.

I have been blessed

The Angel must have come to me once
in some dream, maybe when I was 7 or 8.
I wrestled with Him, heard Him cry in the wind
as He surrendered and disappeared into the night-time Southerly.

I heard Him. The sounds of poetry, that only Gods
or their Messengers can speak, and all my life since
I have tried to find those words again,
the ones which lifted me from a moonlit garden to the stars;

blessed to be a poet, not for fame or gain, but to have
heard those harmonies in the night-time struggle, the wind
across the roof, the moon across my bed, my father dead,
and poetry the message I wrestled from the dark.

Vegetable Thoughts

As a kid I dreamt of other places,
hung over the fence by the surf-shed
staring into the horizon
seeing Chile's Andes in its clouds,
blind to future million-dollar views at my feet.

Now I hang out at the pub,
stuck in the one place,
sessile as a spud,
happy in the dirt I've dug myself into.

But given seven days of rain,
and now the sun,
green dreams reach out to other times
and stir in that always balmy wind
that is the past, up there where tendrils
of memory stir in the air, drawing life
from condensing, coalescing skeins of feelings,
which settle into melting mountains of thought,
making eyes in the dark of winter soil.

The curse of writing

The set essay, theme, debate
for or against, argument and proof —
I could never do it:
like writing a will, it all had to do
with a world I would not be part of,
a world of angles and equity
where both sides of the equation
finally balance out — in death.
But writing is process
and process is reality
—as they taught us in the 1930s—
and there is no end — or beginning,
merely the transition from imaginary point to point
in continual flux
that constellation of the word
the galactic sentence
and universal poem
a form of speech
but frozen into the geometry of print
a pyramid of meaning
no one understands anymore
its apex pointing doggedly
to the way out to God
or some other being greater than our animal self.
Writing like fire is a lousy master
its promises are immediate and sustaining
but its residue is ash and a cold morning—
the frosty welcome Adam found
when he woke after his accident.
After he named the animals,
writing was his cushion, and the pillow
where his last sighs were smothered.

Deep Structures

Is there an image there before the word?
  Is the slot there before the filler?

What is the syntax of a string of beads?
  The knot that ends the sentence?

Where is the silence of the pearl,
  but in the pause drilled through its centre?

How is the verb which puts it all in motion,
  tied up in space and time into a circle?

Why are the colours clauses strung
  in looping patterns of boxed meaning?

When does the subject affirm the predicate,
  but in the clasp which makes the closure?

And what is a poem but the subject made the object?

Symmetry

in the chaos of my early senses
I knew there was some kind of order—

the night sky, star-fish, cactus blossom

but what it was I didn't know:
in early adolescence, God perhaps,

but then came chaos of a different kind
yet also at that time was work

helping out, part-time, with standpipes,
hoses, cables and electrics, engines, chemistry,

and there it was, the hint of order:

male and female hose connections,
positive and negative poles,
right-hand, left-hand threads,
clockwise and anti-clock,

rotations 90, 180, 270 degrees
and gears and molecules would mesh
crystals transform and grow

there was a vital order,
a fearful symmetry

and then I found poetry

The Comfort of Clouds

a drifting 5 knot southerly
autumnal quiet,
after a restless night
the sea breathes deeply,
a baby cries

along the horizon
from north to south
the eastern rim
of this street's visible world:
the clouds—
      sea's other shape,
its liquid soul, taking on forms
that start our dreaming,
suggest the tessellated patterns
we stretch on empty domes of air,
write ancient sky-blue myths upon
the inside of our bubble planet;

clouds are our daily comfort—
the unseen nurse of night
who makes shadows
on moonlit walls of water,
the day-time wash of watery white
which gives size and distance
to infinity

they guide our minds
and soak our bodies,
they are our link
between pure air
and elemental mud,
they change the prose of weather
into poetry.

A Blondin moment

On the back of the gas bill in pencil:
"if poetry is half thought, half feeling,
then how to wobble between the two
on the high wire of a waking dream,

find a sentence, stuff it with an image,
then hold it across your chest
as the Niagara of the moment
pours urgently beneath your feet? —

once you start you can't go back
after the first step — the confident rush
of syllables, sure feet, no doubt
what goes before what, draws you on —

until in the roar and mist half way across
leaving the initial thought behind
sensing the heart beat ahead
the quick breath of climax and closure

shimmering in the radiant halo
of a gauzy sun, you know it's the goal
that's always been before you,"
but what if you stuff it up? —

put the wrong foot forward,
the awkward beat, changed metre,
false voice, wrong tone and
you lose the lot that's so carefully balanced,

so you have to press on in a gathering rush
the sentence cradled in your arms
at a run towards that other side
of pure feeling you cannot see:

the final firm foothold
you know is in the inarticulate
haze that marks the other bank,
"the last gasp of relief at another safe passage."

Afternoon drinkers

Maitland, Clubhouse Hotel, 1530, 11/1/08

dog days in the slow tropics of the suburbs
afternoon TV, C&W muzak,
the Races, mumbling solitaries,
a loud conversation of two retirees
neither of whom listen to each other,
the lone overweight woman
with schooner in hand
and wedding ring on finger
still in black from the supermarket shift
dreams at the soaps while
someone with a biro dreams at his

The Poet considers her approaching death

i

as an angel : as a girl : myself
and mirrors from my earliest memories
mother's eyes black rings with flecked emerald
bright as grass and touched with sun-brown

but then I saw only colours, words were
the stranger come into the kitchen, nasty and rude
who blocked the sun on the tiles and gave
the air a frost over the oven cooking cake

but still an angel : at night in the room's corner
and outside the moon and morepoke and inside
the combing buzz of mother's voice before the lights went out
bag dark I still saw lights and knew the angel in kind
a warm blanket rolled round me and picked up
carried into another room and slept warm with her

ii

as a dog : mother always had one, a familiar
lion to unicorn, emu to kangaroo, my fabulous beast
who made my first dream, hairy-chinned airedale
tweed-suited and rough : I woke screaming, but in love

days were tug-of-war and torment, barks then growl,
sandal-stink of dog tracked in the lounge, fido
never put off, and when I went to school he pined
then died, off-stage, by bait, trap, or plot

I wondered for a while and had my dream :
kennelled in the night I learnt to sleep one ear up
twitching with flea dreams and running the fence

all through primary school, mother's mate, nice,
house-trained and predictable, clean nose and pants, but
the rough hairs itched and I snarled myself awake

iii

as a girl I counted clothes, knew every
combination, content of each drawer and place,
how they would touch and what the colours said
pond smooth ripples of weave and patterned swell
the fabric hung upon me where I grew
night by night, and my secret inside was outside
in my skin fine-grained as hour-glass sand
I was a mermaid with a tail cut on the bias

that's how I looked back on her : as a girl :
clothed to nakedness, teeth and bright eyes
in the back row no different from the other faces
in school uniform except my skin turned out
and the badges of blood spotted my face as well

iv

as a bride : I accompanied the piano
from mother's house to His, scales inside my head
and I loved it : morning sun on the trellis, the steam
from the first cup of tea, playing to myself at three

then years it went untuned, when Todd turned five
the last, I used the endowment to make it concert pitch,
equal temperament, marriage of accidentals, black
notes I wrote, fingers tapping the keys, poems like scales

and no one listened : it was background noise, blocks
of type, chords of wood, chopped out of silence, I
tried to tell him, he listened, but heard only music

my curse I brought with me was always to sing in tune
the formal stanza, rhyme, the counterpoint of speech,
rehearsing myself until the scales became eyes

v

mum's the word, first word said by baby
and baby boy made me Mum, unlike my own,
or Alanna will be : mum begins every poem
and without her lips fills every silence, um :
sounds unwinding from the cot like cochineal
in a rainbow cake, they grew into their sentences,
pilled and felted, passed from one to the other,
each explaining how this season followed the other

strange creatures who said things I'd never heard
new and different, like our change in money,
same value different sense, and so I wrote
in their mother tongue, dipped in honey and gall,
my mother's thoughts, my soul, their words
so they would understand their parent's baby talk

vi

older women, it is written, still write with their juices :
I know mine, old companion, usually named male,
who doesn't come round anymore, so, fond farewell,
I dry out like an apple, with juice still at the core

is the muse male? pick you up then drop you like that
when you've done the job : blood, come, and melt run
down your leg, like sap from a wounded tree,
Daphne and Syrinx, woody victims for poets to play on

but I still dream of cacti, kitchen ledge garden
which flowered vulva, crimson with cellophane petals, gifts,
once unwrapped not treasured, the daily miracle ignored :

give me a beating heart and burning face, I want
to lose myself, and not see when I look in the salt scald
of the bathroom mirror, the wrinkled skin of Granny Smith

vii

as for myself : the cancer was not unexpected, shadows
are cast by everything except ghosts and grails
an X-ray of the lady of shallot would show the same —
that's where I live, not in the mirror of my cell

and what is it but growth gone wrong, dying of birth :
HeLa's immortal cell is art not life, her cervix
opening to the trump of doom — ars longa if you
have slaves, rich friends, but me : I have myself

so long to find her, this subtle friend who paid the bills
and never took the credit, who I met first time last year,
my real self, the germ within my mother's egg, so short
to know her, so long without her, but now we talk non-stop
through fogs of pain, and by the bright light of death
I read what she has written : courage, you were the prince as well.

Fado

It's late Spring and the claret ash is dead.
It tried: parsley sprouts from a skinny branch,
some clotted seaweed on a patch of trunk,
the rest, an X-ray of an anatomised lung.

It dominates the garden, and my perch where I write.
I could moralise my age and state, dream on Valéry's
Jeune Parque, a virgin Fate, weeping bloody tears
as she cuts roots and hacks at my life-line.

I could think of a lot of poems, and not write mine.
Item: Hölderlin on the Fates seen in his youth
before madness claimed him—in that short Spring he bragged
'Once I lived like the Gods, no more is needed.'

Now there's a moral for our times. But back to this:
the poem for a season from a poet past three score and ten.
If I were Chinese there wouldn't be a problem, Li Bai
would use some Mah Jong characters and all is set in aspic.

But not in the deadly prose of English which has its music,
yet not like muscular German, or hot-and-sweaty French,
labial Italian, or my favourite, smokey Portuguese,
my flypaper poetry sticks to the page and doesn't fly.

Never mind. Late Spring, the Fates, the vegetative world in heat:
there's music in the air, late afternoon, warmth in the sun,
some cooler air from the lazy north—all's well—
the pen is in my hand and all I have to do is write,

be my own Fate, and let the biro be a knife.

emergent conditions

so you wait for inspiration

once it was a goddess's warming touch
or an angel's burning coal on the tongue

these days somewhere in chthonic folds
of the cerebral cortex apollo's light hides

in a slight gradient of charge just waiting
to spark, like today, my grandmother's birthday

out of the dark cell of memory, its lipid shell
containing that one charge, comes a current

of comfort: an instant of smell, touch and tears

poetry is

for Bobby

nothing as precise as a gear wheel
nor as clear as orthogonal projections
not even as true as a sand-mould
cooling white-hot metal to a flower

poetry does none of that
it is the road map of invisible cities
the private mysteries of broken symmetries
structures which evaporate to nothing
when you hold them up to the real world

yet it is chemistry:
'nothing is made, only changed'
there is only star dust and
phase transitions of the mind
solids that are flux,
gas you can touch
transmutations

that other periodic table
we use when we dream

prince of darkness

for Larry

poised with the screwdriver
over a sixty-year-old Lucas light switch
I pause

one false move and this delicate assembly
might fly apart, spring-loaded
trap for the unwary

and in this poised pause I think

life is a self-assembly of inert pieces
drawn together by unequal forces
and held in balance by tension

death is the disassembly of things
thrown apart by the spring-loaded
force of entropy and scattered in chaos

so this little bundle of bakelite and steel
is much like the hand which holds it—
tiny pools of order held together

by the unstable surface tension of Will
and sooner rather than later
that Will will turn on itself and tinker with the bits

until like a jack in the box all is cast
once more across the face of the waters
and darkness settles over all creation

the mechanics of verse

they were not wrong those older poets

verse should slide as easily as white metal
on a crank, smooth as a cylinder wall, fierce
in its beat and noise, terrify with consonantal friction,
have vowels which open and softly sigh, valves of the soul,
or belt and hammer, anglo-saxon tappets
in a valve train of oily alexandrines,
then put it all into motion, regulated,
ticking over with rhyming precision

instead of this unsyncopated raggedness of free verse:
timing, syntax only, and cadence and breath
from an over-rich carburettor, roaring,
back-firing, its oily exhaust smoking immediate presence
which turns heads, but leaves hearts unmoved

The Shed

ut pictura poesis

to make something out of water,
sculpt the moment,
freeze music,
let words hang
like late season peaches,
set that mark on blankness,
rule lines,
put into play

out of all that bangs
on the corrugated shed of self
make out of that fluid field
of wave on sand something
with those tools
which hang on shadows of themselves
like these thoughts
which will themselves into shapes

Feeler Gauge

leaves of steel rice paper

a book of absences
engraved with distances

of those necessary gaps in things
through which sense disappears

that space between edges
where mind stops and feeling takes over

an intuitive spark
at twenty thou between poles

the relief between percussive
surfaces of teeth or tappet

where only air and touch
can carry force

in these dark places
only the thin skin of steel

can bring out into the light
the incarnation of nothing

Vyse

In an uncertain world
it holds the object like a retriever
firm, unmoving, ready
to cut, file or drill

place without doubt
jaws fixed in a death grip
squeezed to their limits
it makes things handleable

resistant metals yield
shape emerges
fluid plans become fact
in a world held fast

Timing Chain

the endless loop
linking all in lock step
creating the harmony
of valves and pistons
it mimics the universe
models your heart

but not the mind

Carpenter's Rule

Unfold it like a bride—
box-wood limbs fit
each brass joint
into one long blonde line

the units of division
match each perfect part:
first her foot, then thumb
marked into fractions

the inch's calculus
of sixteenths, thirty-seconds,
sixty-fourths, the whole
a yard of beauty

stretching from nose to fingertip.
An ell of samite shot
with golden thread
her arms extended to embrace

all that you plan to do:
the four by two of pine
ready for saw and plane
clamped to the bench's block.

Out of it will come
those ideal angles of a box
square and right unseen in any tree
to hold her sheets and towels.

Brace and Bit

Bent like a broken arm
a sock mushroom on top
the bit bites and bores
into wood scribing a hole

the chiselled auger brings up
shavings of pine
smelling of forest and wind
they curl around the deepening shaft

out of something it makes nothing
absence to be filled
by the dowel of thought
and the glue of passion

all your weight braced
into the fine point of change
to break up life's order
to fit the purpose of the mind

Spirit Level

pick up the oiled wood
grooved and shaped to hold
the brass cage
inside is the improbable angel
the essence of nothing
which shapes this world
makes surfaces flat
lintels square
walls upright

look, that airy absence
locked in its elemental shroud
slips this way and that
anxious to be gone
but unable
trapped in our space
to give us the outline
of a world outside time

Oil Stone

this is the place of limits
where steel finishes and air starts

a line so fine, hairs split
testing its edge

it's also the place of oil
carrier of ambiguity

smearing all detail
aiding the abrasion of thought

until we don't know where
one ends and the other begins

this is the place of vacuum
the ideal tool to make the world

Boilermaker's Hammer

originally a tinker's tool
now it is used on iron
to make that perfect shape
the sphere and cylinder
which holds steam
in a geometry of power

made from its two surfaces
the flat face shiny as pond water
rippled with windy blows
the peen round and smooth
as rolled river stones

where the sledge drives rivets
and the block bends billets
over the anvil, the ball peen
teases form out of the inchoate
seducing metal to our will

ductile then rigid the boiler skin
is pure in form and shape
it shines with hammer blows
and takes strength and purpose
as slag and dross are beaten out

these plates are shaped in the mind
to curve and contain
curtain off and fasten
the wild daughter of fire and water
to put her to work in our quarries and mines

but what of the hammer at rest?
head black as night
the greased hickory shaped to the hand
it hangs in its bracket, a femur
waiting to spring

Bastard File

like life
it's halfway between
coarse and fine

already the rough spots are smooth
but there are those ups and downs
you can see when you sight it
along the light from the clouded window
thick with the swarf of earlier jobs
not one thing or the other
but half hill, half valley
the metal shines with the promised end
the ideal surface in which you can see your face

just now it's still opaque
waiting for more work
that constant abrasion
between effort and resistance
nature and perfection

Tyre Lever

on a bicycle tyre you can use
a greased screwdriver
even the blunt side of a hacksaw blade

but nothing does the job better than
an old spoon handle's curved return
to slip the rubber selvage from its rim

but a car tyre's carcass calls
for an instrument
capable of inflicting death

weapon of the night
steel femur waved at strangers
beyond the rim of light

run it up under the bead
make the circle's blackness
sit and grip—force

the whole round world of torment
into shape with the lever's lunge
and bang! inflation fills the void

Nuts and Bolts (and Shackles)

There in the jam jars and tobacco tins
of sheds are the fasteners of years,
put by to tie down some future need:

mild steel, high tensile, BSF, AF, Whitworth
thread gauges fine as nit combs
nuts domed and castellated

a rubble of short shanked bolts and nyloc nuts
mating pairs unscrewed generations before
waiting reunion at some latter day

when will it come out of the darkness
that moment when the shed is sold
and the future throws up the roller door

and no bolt or shackle will hold
this world of brass or iron—
gone like the gold flake and preserves

Retractable Rule

an infinitely extendible finger
it reaches out to the far corner
bends, and curls across the floor

back to the centre
where the mark
tells us where we are

press with the thumb
it disappears into itself:
it is the mind's homunculus

measure of all we are in space
and like time
it springs back into ourselves

ready to reach out and
touch the walls and corners
of where we live

Paint

It grows skin just like us
yet escapes it to touch up
the inappropriate:
leaves rings on cement
skeined gloves to the elbows
and smears on knobs
so years later burnt orange
still smoulders on a black bench top

that liquid centre which sets
its mark on surfaces
transforming spherical to plane
lies sealed in darkness until
the lid is lifted and light
floods in to colour its nature
and thought splashes out
to cover everyday walls with wonder

Screw driver

engine of the evolved nail
Nature's spiral, Archimedes' screw
which can lift water, drive ships
and hold together the world
against the level of gravity

simple shaft, cousin of the stick,
our first tool, it carries the twist,
rotation of the wrist, mind's mimic
of all fallen motion deflected from
the straight line of initial cause,
without which nothing would hold

Wire-stripper

neatly the curved blades
cut through the sheath

the inner line untouched
the braided band entire

do it with razor-blade or knife
and half its virtue is lost

threads hang, strength frayed
and contact broken

only the proper tool will work
blessed by design and use

passed down from father to son
to expose the golden core

to tin and flux, then melt,
make solid, firm, and only connect

Funnel

Most enigmatic of shapes
the cone:
both circle and triangle

capable of modelling
the fluid space
we swim in,

it puts limits
on all we see—

orbit, iris, pupil
all drain to one point:
watertight word or number.

Ram in the cork,
or screw down
on that mercurial presence,

put it away to decant
in some other place and time
otherwise everything is everywhere.

Hoses and Pipes

of all tools
the ones with the most difficult task:
to tame water

induce
in Nature's plastic form
our swirls and twists

create a circus
from gravity in fountains and siphons
or chthonic sewers

translate
a spring from here to there
without spilling a word

and mimic
our own waste and generation
in spigots and taps

but washers fail
and hoses split
leaks and floods fill night-time dreams

and whatever mind can make
is levelled in water's play
by rules we know but will not follow

Glass-cutter

Too like a pen—
I could never master it:

scribe that line
a frosty trace
across a pool of glass

break the liquid surface
hear it crack as the line
ends and another starts

with that one tap
make the shape to fit
the empty frame

seal off the wind and rain
bend light and deaden sound
and make the limits of the shed

Time and Motion

Internal weather

there's high cirrus today
a high altitude westerly
has set corduroy ripples across the sky

on the coast the gales have stopped
tides have calmed and across the flats
corduroys of sand and mud

earth and sky obey the same rules
common energies and forces push and pull
there are no angels in these crystal spheres

our dull sublunary world and the seventh heaven
are bound by Newton's chains and fluxions—
I would that I could say the same about internal weather

unpredictable, moody, tropical, arctic,
doldrums and fevered straits, dipole dislocations,
winds circulate within my globe

follow no season, rage and still,
its waves toss up on rocks, bore up quiet estuaries,
then die in slothful calm

there is no logic, no universal law
except the deep structure of chaos
and consciousness riding those cresting waves

inside the bubble

imagine you're there:

the walls shimmering with the moment
an instant as it breaks and reforms
always that shimmering moment

fluid but vacant, it's Time, motion,
the continual present, the never fixed
of sliding tensors, collapsing, reforming

the bubble is the wall of cause and effect,
the mind's window and mirror
self-made, the story we tell ourselves:

first the bubble breathed out as sound
joined with others, unfolding
into the word, bonding into sentences

then the story, making the greater bubble, Time,
which enfolds us in the future, the past,
but always fixed is the physical real

froth of the vacuum, continually springing into being
then disappearing, points which are fields,
the eternally present Now, the shimmering wall

Giving up the Sea

It's a different life far from the sea:

no sign or sound sequestered so far inland
once or twice a year you can smell it
on some updraft escaped from the escarpment
echoes of that noise and trouble from next door
the drunken father's southerly buster
mum's day-long nagging nor-easter
and the occasional aunt's dry sarcasm from the west
they're just memories here in the calm of
silent frost and sound-proof snow

but every so often after an afternoon of stunning heat
lolling at the council's pool of tamed and treated water
line storms of hail and thunder will clear the streets
like a cranky publican at closing time

then indoors with the shaking dog you smell
clear as cungewoi and kelp the salty taste of ozone
struck out of the heavens by a flash of light

Story Time

motion is an illusion

there are only discrete packets of the real
lumps of matter, stones which are only
toe-bruising to the human mind

the rest is fiction

Newton's laws are narrative
and there are other stories
with different endings and beginnings

all because of TIME which is
a human construct of predictability
guessing the story to come

all science is predictive narrative
like our vision which sees only change
ignoring the rest as static and no threat

that's the problem, time is a story
which makes sense for us of inert lumps of matter
so that we see trees instead of wood

like today's 30 knot westerly
which tears a branch off a Norfolk Pine
and sends it flapping onto the pavement

a moment ago it was a breathing
organ pulsing with sap
now it is wood in the gutter, mute and still

and the mind makes narrative of before and after
seeing cause and effect where there is only change
Hume was right, only stone and wood are real

the rest is hypothesis, the story we tell the kids
as we tuck them in at night—and then they dream,
where mind in its wild flight roars like a wind

Inside-out and Back-to-front

For years I've relied on others to tell me
as I get to the front door
"That jumper's on the wrong way round,
it's inside-out and back-to-front".
So easy to become confused
swimming your way into arms and head-hole
as to where you will come out,
often into that looking-glass world
that adults find so distressing;
yet this is where I have spent most my life
unsure of right or left, up, down, north or south
invariably the world's poles have reversed
while I've been under wool hauling
my way through cable stitch and raglan sleeves.
But logic and maths I know can demonstrate
these rotations of reality are at base the same;
strange then that metaphor, syllogism's enemy,
should prove so powerful, showing
the inside-out as not the same but different,
holding within its yoke two unlike possibilities,
as compassed knots which make closures on a needle
unravel once the rigid designator's removed
and the jumper becomes the thread
which led me through this labyrinth.

Consciousness is a window of old glass

Rippled and stretched
the trees and sky
bend in the stilled water
of the vertical pond:

outside becomes inside
when cataracts of light
stream into the
the cave behind,

then, squeezed by the lens
into a bubble hemisphere,
mapped and graded
on an inverse globe,

it lives by the moment:
shape, colour, movement,
silent pictures forming
dissolving reforming—

the stream thins,
becomes drops, each
a silver trail, a rope of beads,
a head to tail circle of famine;

cold sweat on the rattled pane
tracking to some deeper centre,
they run to where you live,
slump into focus, and be.

consciousness

waiting for inspiration
from the flux of reality
in this room of people

whether the glance,
the drawn breath, this mark
can make a gift to others

of this moment where space
is real and time is not, art,
closed fist around the butterfly

yet in another moment it will
be memory, where time is real
and space the illusion, the dream

fluid with feeling not thought
our only trace of being alive
wavering like lake bed weeds

Alternative Science

'It was aesthetics rather than science. I was looking for Beauty not Truth.'
Social Psychologist accused (successfully) of fraudulent data

so Keats was wrong:
there is no equals sign
between Truth and Beauty

Truth can be ugly,
Beauty a lie,
that's what
the twentieth century taught us,

but the lesson is forgotten
in the twenty-first.

Purge the outliers,
get rid of the inconvenient,
massage away the weighty distribution
in the wrong place:

give us this day that set of beautiful numbers
which abolish want
and clean the streets of crime

the unemployed invisible,
the black and needy unquantifiable,
teenage mothers and asbestos widows
beyond the pale of graphs

all banished from our perfect kingdom,
the harmony and beauty of wish
more real than the stubborn rock of fact.

The Beach

in the moment

here we are at the beach:
the space we have had in our heads all winter
the sand in our inner eyes
each time we surface from day dreams
the beach where everything gathers together
then falls apart
constant energy its own end
the edge, mystery of limits
phase transition
the only place where geology happens in real time

against entropy

first principles

just past the solstice
the tide is slack
still water —
the only change
wind's surface glitter:
fresnel patterns
incoherence
of fluid and light

it's the glitter of motion
time, sensed only by me
and the pelican on his stump
a coherence of before and after
sentient beings

able to fly
and write

the region air

and so the pelican flies

wings riding the corrugated air
every bump and hollow making
that liquid nothingness visible

while I write, making the visible
flux of table and paper into
the nothingness of words,

the pelican's wings trace a true measure
while my words drop from a solitary quill

a halcyon moment

that syntax of flight
as the pelican moves
from air to water

from one element to another,
noun to verb, to brood
on the face of the waters

makes more sense of peace
than all this restless wrestle
with words and sounds

trying to cage elemental forces
into some form of meaning
called life which really is just

the calm after the storm

pelican : poem

to break that surface tension
of meaning and get free
into the aether of pure feeling

involves using earth-bound feet
to walk on water and rise out of
the pluck of everyday comfort

into the whispy filaments, clouds
of hot and cold, and feel them
through each feathered finger

sliding, rising, falling without thought
just as words tumble around us
pushing us up, holding us down

until the eye catches a sign, a hook,
back in that world of watery sense
and we are back, planing on glitter

to rest, hands full of quicksilver

beer glass weather

what if things aren't falling apart?
but flying together:
sticking in greasy lumps
making washing-board striations
and strung lines of lacey cloud
in the sky   in the petri dish
in rain on the asphalt path
the weather inside my beer glass?

all around I feel the fizz of being—
energy, the microwaves of the big bang
still shaking everything into new patterns of being

there is a general stickiness everywhere:
the old couple holding hands walking through the RSL park
where a Mark IV torpedo sits calmly under the cabbage palms
full of itself and its intricate purpose—
the duck head-down charging its inferiors,

we're all iron filings shaken into this moment's pattern
adhering, signing, speaking out of the buzz of force and field

this isn't running down, it's merely changing,
changing like the tide every day, a deep order
which throws out blossoms of beauty for us to feel,
the sense that, like us, something
has come from what we thought was nothing

but really is that fizz of life in everything

In time of plague

1 march 2020 number one

who can tell the singer from the song in
        order at key west?
and other confusions of half-
        remembered poems –
there must be better ways
        of looking at the world.

item:
        norfolk island pines in the park
inverted toilet brushes
        you can't see them in this poem
perhaps you can feel them
        pipe-cleaners of the soul
pointing sky-wards to revelations
        we no longer believe in

or the stand of paper-barks beyond them
        blanched asparagus trunks
in the setting sun, dark green

curly mop-head tops
sweeping the floor of heaven

and so the echoes go:
            interference patterns
from a direct gaze upon the world —
            but what if the world is
only echoes of a deeper song
            vibrating from the string of time
and all is echo and I narcissus
            a poem of a poem?

but then there is the silence of the green
            beneath the trees
still and inviting, waiting, waiting
            for the idle to tread warily
into its silent peace

In time of plague

1 march 2020 number two

in time of plague we mark
            the first day of autumn
the drought has ended   the fires are out
            crimson banksias glow in the greenery
rainbow parakeets thread colour
            through the hakea
the exhausted world of summer smoulders

it is the drowsy numbness of exhaustion
            after the last wild party
of broken glass and ruined bodies
            from forty summers of excess and greed

156

now the sickness of the soul shambles
　　　　out of the middle kingdom
darkness falls from the air
　　　　our leaders prove shams
our idols and gods cheap goods

and I am sick, Lord, I must die

seasonal ledger

the last week before daylight saving:
there is a dislocation between body and light—
the tides carry on, the dawn chorus is the same

but the late afternoon is not in balance –
the skies are empty waiting for the stars,
the water bluer, the moon has risen too early

and now it sits like the sun at noon
at half past three – the kids are out,
so are spring grevilleas, their bees heading for home—

it's not the world that's wrong—it's me,
wound up, screwed to the limit, wringing
my hands but telling the wrong time.

I've been spending not saving, like all of us,
sure that there is no grim reaper, or bailiffs
to turf us out of our comfortable digs,

but here they are: the tide gnawing the front yard,
the fire at the back fence, and the black bat
of plague sitting on the midnight bed-stead

and tomorrow all our debts will be one hour sooner

Frangipani and Doves

In suburban gardens by a beach
children train their senses by sound and smell.
These are not the wide spaces of sight:
steel-rimmed horizons of noon-light sea
or the hazy albedo of sea-mist afternoons,
but the enclosed space of fence and shed
reason's map of possession and trade,
the garden beds of planned strangeness
lined out in tile and brick on coastal heath,
and in them on invisible currents come
indelible traces laid down to haunt old age
as memories stronger than any plan or picture,
the smell of frangipani and the sound of doves.

sleepless in the longest night of the year

I saw the sun set

the yachts slack on the turn of the tide
a weight of clouds on the horizon
and the cold rising from the oyster flats

now, wrapped deep in the darkness
among night's weed and mud
I hope my anchor will hold

in this smothering time, rope tight
round the neck of the night, drawn
tighter by the tug of dawn, I toss

on the solid wave of wakefulness
hold my breath against its upswell
then slip into that black trough

where time passes without thought

Inverse square law

the moon has risen
the crow's cold call
from the park's pine top
settles the dark drifts of the river

the sun drowns in the mountain
leaving the moon an earth-quaked
piece of white-washed wall in a dark field

it is second-hand light passed on as charity
for us in the dark, attenuated, diffusing,
meaning radiating out but losing coherence

constellations of words trying to evolve
into heavenly signs, all stretching probability
as the point darkens into ambiguity

Tidal gauge

I reset the tide clock after a month's absence

It had dropped half a tide
counting the tides to the empty house
as the moon went on her usual way—

at the river edge I watch the tide bore in,
a living force and one I live without
home on the tablelands watching the moon

but not feeling that urgent surge, aloof
from that other world of prawns and fish,
away from its pulse of heavenly power which makes

rivers run backward, men mad, and women bleed—
there the moon's pale skin covers the town in quiet,
its sole creek drains one way — into oblivion,

down tormented gullies, heading for home,
the tidal sea — but where is home and time —
a point above change, or deep in its intensity?

and when I come back what will the time be then?

Winds of change

(i.m. Harri Jones 1921-1965)

Nor-easter

late afternoon and the nor-easter
bullies the waterfront trying to turn back
the tide, then dies away …

shadows lengthen, things go slack,
like pulling in the last fish of the day,
I think of you …

then, just as you would get to the float,
then the trace, the lead sinker,
and finally the hook…

no fish, instead those famous lines:
'why do I think of you dead man?'
the drowned man pulled from the deep

the deep of almost sixty years
the encrusted memory, razor-sharp
as an oyster shell ready to draw blood

from these careless feet of windy poetry

Southerly

master of change and drama
the wind is set from the south:
it's near noon and the water dazzles with chop

in all this bluster I'm still here,
an old man on survivor's leave,
while you at 44, to me an old man

when you drowned, suddenly gone
into that dazzlement of change
while I stuck to solid ground

plodded on through each foot-fall year
until now in the noon light and wind
unable to make that next step—

that is the question to be asked:
not to be or not, but to fall into
the blue air of riot and change,

oblivion – which takes your breath away,
and leaves you with nothing left to say.

Westerly

this time last year the sky was red, the air choked,
the tide line littered with ash and burnt leaves
and the wind a steady purge of all our sins

at times like this none of us should be here
driven back to the sea with no time to pack our bags
go home, go back, the wind says, with its fiery tongue

breathing out of angry lungs and a not-so dead heart
westerlies have the mark of Adam reminding us
that this is not the Promised Land but East of Eden,

a place you knew so well: exile, like you wrote
'is a word not lightly said' and New South Wales
was still old Wales, its deserts still those of Old

Testament chapels and their scourging winds,
and 'Back?' was the question you asked yourself,
back to the familiar and internal exile, a hope,

but here, as I know, now another year older,
with the wind bringing showers and soft warmth
in the lull between this continent's fevers

there is no Back, and the wind, like God's anger,
never stops, only drops to a sullen breath,
and then, as all who live on this east coast know,

this westerly drives all before it, one way only, to the sea

lighthouse

surfacing in the shoals of 2 am
breathless from too long in the deep,
terror and teary loss stream off me

the loom of the lighthouse casts
a cold eye on yesterday's mess
the sink, abandoned clothes, paper

unfinished business in a flash
then the dark rip of sleep
sweeps me from the beach again

back into the blanket wave
of the nightly world you've
swum in for nearly fifty years

sailor who couldn't swim
silent poet of the sea and ships
who drowned one careless night

and lives now in shelving rocks
of books, in sea grass memory
waving and tugging in tidal surges

like now as I lie awake and listen
to the swell set into the cliff, a thump
so deep it shakes the bedside glass

old ocean is always there
greedy lover ready to disturb the night
with a dig in the ribs and a cold kiss

so welcome, and now we'll talk of you,
permanent resident with all those others
Palinurus, Li Bai, Lycidas, Shelley, Hart Crane

the realm of poetry where all that's lost
in that moving graveyard of the deep
is locked from sight but not forgotten

you who loved the Quaker Graveyard,
Five Bells, Auden's Icarus, Lucky Jonah
you called yourself, on the beach

and out of the whale, you wrote of a man
born to be drowned cannot be hanged,
good philosophy, but a poor choice.

Chimes at Midnight

out of my senses

privileged to have all of my senses
what do I know?

despite sixty years of glasses, I rely too much on sight,
the perfumes of the night have disappeared with age
the dog knows more about the earthy world than I

and touch? a woman's is different from a man's
and mine is blunted by too many hammer blows,
likewise with taste, which now is only gruel,

but sound—the morning's parliament of fowls
the surf at night from miles away
the nightly murmur of the radio's Taverner mass

console me through my hearing aids,
but there's one more, the sixth sense
of dread and panic, causes one

to touch wood, sound alarms,
taste fear, look out, and smell rats
that no midnight mass can calm

Old papers

"Bring back your lunch papers"
last thing said as you leave the door
off to school after a war and depression—
everything had value
even if it didn't have a price

after the final one had gone,
hung on like a black shrunken apple
in her smelly weatherboard
the last in the block
and only three blocks from the beach

they pulled the lino up
before they put the dozer through
old hands who knew that generation's
distrust of banks,
but found instead of pound notes

old newspapers with columns
cramped with print,
tongue-and-groove wordy ads
for forgotten intimates
lost-long rituals of fetes and socials

stories of those returned from wars
and bitter appeals for those who hadn't,
old papers full of strangers' news
saved and framed with the architect's sketch
to feature on the client's lunch-time patio

Secret Assassinations (after Edward Burra)

secret assassinations
are

the furtive movement of a shadow
in a corner of the bedroom when you wake too early

the half-heard footsteps following you
when you walk the dog

the stranger in the mirror whose face
you shave each morning

the routine of the day with its finger to its lips
cancelling the joy in every moment

the blank stare of disapproval of the bathroom window
when you turn on an early morning light

the mask of faces lined up along the kitchen dresser
of plates waiting to be filled at dinner time

the gravid stove, the fruitful fridge which await your pleasure
conspiring to consume you every day

and all that perishes are not tyrants, nor martyrs
but idle thoughts, half-formed, unwritten

which will be forgotten, struck out by the censor
of the moment, still-born, worse, never quickened,

by the weight of darkness every new dawn brings

Wish you were here …

A postcard from today
to you thirty years away

it's not a bad life
here in our village—
you remember what it was like:
dull but secure
none of the city's edge,
you can see it in this view:

an almost empty afternoon bar
where no one drinks wine
and flannel shirts are all the go,
outside is the usual empty blue
of wall-to-wall sky above
the southern corrugated wall
of the necessary shed
where last night's ice
still lies at three p m

oh yes, it's all the same,
but I wonder if we would be too?

you can see that even in here
the empty sky intrudes
filling the present spaces with the past
each person nursing their drinks
harbours constellations of regrets
which later, after I've put
this in the post, will fill the night sky,
and at three a m
when the frost grips on the coming day

they'll wake wound in flannelled sheets
and for an hour the dark hemisphere
will glitter with their loss, points of pain
when they feel again the forking path
and see their choices shining across the deep

I'll put the stamp on mine and send it now
and know there'll be no reply

Mid April

for years I hardly noticed the seasons—
growing up in the city, on the beach,
I put on sweaters in February, took them off
in July—oblivious to the garden's calendar,
only aware of winds and tides and train timetables

but now each night I check the sky and stars
see how that dusty disk, our sweet vinyl galaxy
tilts through the year. I see the sun rise each week
through different trees and aerials, reach the centre,
or rim, and track back again: spiral music with

spherical harmonies, and unlike a stuck record
the repeating groove may be similar but never the same:
this year's autumn is clear and mild, three years ago
I spent four days cut off without power or internet
in a city swamped by a storm cell, at night I read

Shelley aloud by candlelight and mirror to an empty house.
It seemed poetry then was like weeds which only grew in
    disturbed spaces.
But now, at peace, in light and company I write—
the sun sinking a little later each day making a familiar tune:
that poems not only grow on trees, they also fall from them.

Theaterette

and in the night when you wake
to real and imagined disasters
there in the darkness, pushing past you

roughly excusing themselves intent
on that better seat, crushing your legs,
and making insincere and muffled excuses

is that audience to the newsreel of your life
filling in a few vacant hours from the bright light
of their own lives, they watch your grainy truth

now monstrously magnified with no sense of plot
unedited rushes straight from the subconscious
until, realising they are back to where they came in,

they push past again and disappear into the daylight

Sunset

and the clouds are mother-of-pearl
and we are inside the oyster shell
of gritty earth and the crusted cave of heaven

this orb of gas and charge
which keeps us safe in the wild currents
of our local solar estuary

but here on earth and next to water
we share flux and firmness
feet drawn to an iron centre, heads in the clouds

let the sun set and the moon rise—
around us dance the milky colours
of change and fixture, enamels

of the moment in our cloistered cell

The better half — of half a lifetime

(for Caroline)

the river at peace

turn of the tide

soon all will flow out
to the far heads, the estranging sea

but for the moment the bay is full

boats idle, wind still

you are my full tide

the flood that covers
all the clotted growth, the scummy smear
of all those low tide years

my anchor and my rest

Acknowledgements

I have been fortunate to have had the support of a number of editors and poets over the years. Max Harris, Geoffrey Dutton, Judith Wright, Alec Hope, Les Murray, Louis Simpson, John Leonard, and my current publisher David Musgrave, and to all of them, alive and dead, I am profoundly grateful. Without the help of Jack Bedson I would have found the process of selecting these poems impossible. He is a true friend for wading through the wrack of ages. The literary scene in Armidale for many years kept me active, especially the friendship of Tony Bennett, Tony Lynch, and Michael Sharkey, and I thank the city and the University for the fifty years I spent in the 'Athens of the North'. Finally, I would like my family, sons Larry and Bobby, and my wife Caroline, for the times they have had to suffer from someone deep in what Yeats called 'excited reverie'.

Appendix: Audio Recordings

Each of the following QR codes links to a recording of the author reading the poem.

Aeneid Book VI

p. 105

Bastard File

p. 132

Boilermaker's Hammer

p. 131

Brace and Bit

p. 129

Carpenter's Rule

p. 128

The Comfort of Clouds

p. 111

Deep Structures
p. 109

The dying fire (in mid-winter)
p. 79

Feeler Gauge
p. 126

Frangipani and Doves
p. 158

Funnel
p. 137

Glass-cutter
p. 138

Hoses and Pipes
p. 137

Nuts and Bolts (and Shackles)
p. 133

Oil Stone
p. 130

Paint
p. 135

Poetry Is
p. 135

prince of darkness
p. 124

Retractable Rule
p. 134

Screw driver
p. 135

The Shed
p. 126

sleepless in the longest night
p. 158

Spirit Level
p. 130

Symmetry
p. 110

Timing Chain
p. 128

Tyre Lever
p. 133

Underworld, Orphic Meditations
p. 100

ut pictura poesis
p. 126

Vyse
p. 127

Wire-stripper
p. 136

www.ingramcontent.com/pod-product-compliance
Lightning Source LLC
Chambersburg PA
CBHW030831090426
42737CB00009B/967